Table of Contents

MW01089543

Step 1: Clothing 7

Step 2: Licensing & Hunter Safety 12

Step 3: Gun Types 15

Step 4: Gun Accessories..21

Step 5: What Else to Bring Hunting 24

Step 6: Where to Hunt...28

Step 7: How to Get Permission to Hunt Private Land..31

Step 8: Finding Public Land to Hunt..36

Step 9: Prepping for Your Hunt...39

Step 10: Hunting Seasons 42

Step 11: Time of Day for Squirrel Hunting 45

Step 12: Identifying Squirrel 48

Step 13: Looking for Signs of Squirrels 53

Step 14: Squirrel Hunting with the "Still" Method 57

Step 15: Stalking Squirrel..61

Step 16: Party Hunting for Squirrels 66

Step 17: Squirrel Calling..70

Step 18: Shooting 72

Step 19: Retrieving Your Squirrel..78

Step 20: Squirrel Cleaning 80

Step 21: Time to Enjoy Your Squirrel!...82

Final Words...84

The Key to Squirrel Hunting Success is Found Right Here in this Book.

In this book I teach you all of the essentials you need to know to achieve the best results possible in the sport of squirrel hunting. It is my goal to save you the pain, heartache and lost time that many hunters experience when they participate in this sport.

Example of one of the Images in this Book:

Overview:

- To begin, I will review the equipment you need including clothing, firearms and accessories.

- Next I cover where to hunt, how to get permission to hunt private land and detailed hunting instructions.

- The final portion of this book covers shooting techniques and what to do after you shoot.

Attention All Struggling Squirrel Hunters...

"Finally A Comprehensive Resource for Squirrel Hunting All In One Place. Never Has It Been So Easy To Start Squirrel Hunting!"

What are the Common Mistakes Squirrel Hunters Make?

1. Using the wrong type of gun

2. Not understanding squirrel habits

3. Using poor shooting techniques

How Do You Avoid These Mistakes?

In this book I will equip you with all the knowledge you need to immediately experience success in this sport. Put these lessons into action to avoid or discontinue making the common mistakes.

Who Can Benefit from This Book?

I provide relevant information for squirrel hunters of any experience level:

- People curious about this sport

- People ready to get started in this sport

- Novice squirrel hunters

- Squirrel hunters struggling for success

Now let's get started...

Step 1: Clothing

Appropriate Clothing for Squirrel Hunting

The temperature during squirrel hunting season can vary greatly so it is important to dress appropriately for the time of year that you will be hunting squirrels. In most areas squirrel hunting is done in the fall and early winter so you need to have clothes that will allow you to remain warm during these cooler times.

Additionally, in most small game hunting situations you need to have blaze orange clothing covering the top half of your body. This is to make it easy for other hunters to see you when you are hunting.

Squirrel hunting season commonly overlaps with other small game hunting seasons, including pheasant hunting and even deer hunting, so there will be lots of hunters around at this time. You absolutely want to be sure to follow the laws for your area concerning what to wear so you are visible to other hunters. But even if it is not a requirement in your area, I would recommend wearing blaze orange to increase visibility.

Clothing that you will want to have:

- Blaze orange coat, or a blaze orange vest (with or without coat, depending on temperature)

- Blaze orange baseball hat or stocking cap

- Thick jeans in the fall, snow style hunting pants in the winter

- Long underwear, depending on the temperature

- Gloves, depending on the temperature

- Boots

- Wool Socks, depending on the temperature

Blaze Orange Coat or Blaze Orange Vest

Depending on where you live and the time of year that you are hunting for squirrels, you will probably encounter a large range of temperatures. Temperatures for early season hunting could easily be 60-70 degrees. In contrast, temperatures in December could be below zero.

You can choose from two different ways to ensure that you have the top half of your body covered with blaze orange. You can either use a blaze orange hunting jacket or you can just use a blaze orange hunting vest.

If you already have a camouflage or other warm jacket, I would recommend just purchasing a blaze orange hunting vest to go over your coat. Vests can be very inexpensive, typically around $20 or $30. It would only make sense to invest in a blaze orange coat if you do not already have a coat to use or if you could also use it for other hunting that you do,

The other nice thing about having a hunting vest though is that you can use it on the warmer days over a long sleeve shirt or sweatshirt. There are many days that I hunt for squirrel where all I need is a long sleeve shirt, and the vest makes it easy to get into legal hunting apparel. When looking for a hunting vest you also might want to keep in mind that it is convenient to have one with a pocket for game. We will discuss this further in the section title "What Else to Bring Hunting."

Blaze Orange Baseball Hat or Stocking Hat

On the warmer fall days, a blaze orange baseball hat is what I use for my squirrel hunting trips. These hats ensure that I have enough orange on to be seen by fellow hunters. Additionally, the baseball hat style permits my ears to be uncovered allowing me to listen for squirrels without any sound loss.

When the temperatures dip as the season progresses, you may want to convert over to a blaze orange stocking hat. Again, the blaze orange increases visibility to the rest of your hunting party and any other hunters that may be in the area.

Stocking hats provide plenty of warmth as the year gets colder. They might dampen a little bit of the sound as you try to listen for squirrels, but at this time of year it is usually more important to stay warm. Some stocking hats convert into facemasks which is nice if you are "still" hunting for squirrels (meaning you are sitting in one spot and waiting for them versus actively moving around and looking for them) or if it is a very cold day.

Thick Jeans in the Fall, Warm Hunting Style Snow Pants in the Winter

Warm fall days call for a thick pair of jeans. Jeans allow you plenty of freedom of movement while they also provide good protection from thorns, branches, fences and other items that you may encounter when you are squirrel hunting.

I recommend not wearing brand new jeans that you want to keep nice for your other activities. It is best to pull out that old pair of jeans from your closet.

When hunting in the later season you may need to put on some type of warm hunting snow pants over your jeans. These also come in blaze orange if you really want the extra visibility, but most regulations only call for your top half to be covered with blaze orange.

Long Underwear

The need for these will depend on the time of year and how active you plan to be when hunting. For those days that are very cold outside, if you do not plan to be real active while hunting, you can add a level of comfort by wearing long underwear.

Most of the squirrel hunting I do is active hunting. This means that I am always moving around and trying to find squirrels that are in the trees or running on the ground. The constant movement tends to keep me warm enough so I do not need the long underwear.

However, if you are planning on doing "still" hunting where you sit in one place and wait for squirrels to come out of hiding, long underwear is recommended.

Gloves

Sometimes in the early season I elect to go squirrel hunting without gloves. As long as the weather permits I prefer not to wear gloves.

When the temperature gets colder I do put on a pair of gloves, but I prefer lightweight gloves even on the very cold days. This is because the lightweight gloves can actually be worn while shooting and they still provide some extra warmth. I do not like thick gloves as I do not want to have to remove them in order to pull the trigger of my gun.

However, if you plan on doing any "still" hunting, then you will most likely want to have a nice pair of warm hunting gloves. Similar to what we discussed with long underwear, "still" hunting will cause you to cool down faster because you are not moving around, so having warm gloves on while you wait for squirrels to come out of hiding is a very good idea.

Boots

Lightweight boots, similar to hiking boots are very nice for the early season. If you are going to be actively going after squirrels, you will want to be able to move quickly to keep up with these fast moving animals. Lightweight boots or active hiking/hunting shoes allow you to move quickly through the woods while still providing protection from branches, rocks, etc.

Also, if you wear heavy hunting boots in warmer temperatures they can cause your feet to sweat and make for an uncomfortable hunt. However, there are times for warm winter hunting boots.

Grab your warm winter hunting boots for the cold days and any mild days that you will be doing a lot of "still" hunting. Having cold toes can quickly turn a fun hunting adventure into a miserable experience.

Wool Socks

In the early season you can get away with just wearing regular socks, however, colder days call for increased protection for your toes. You can find warm wool socks at a reasonable price at your local sporting goods store. Typically, you can get them for about $5-$10 a pair and they will be well worth the money.

Now let's examine licensing and hunter safety…

Step 2: Licensing & Hunter Safety

Get Your Small Game & Applicable Safety Registration

It is important to purchase a hunting license and learn hunting safety prior to heading out for a squirrel hunting adventure. The laws and regulations for hunting are very different from one area to the next. In the majority of cases you will need to purchase some type of hunting license to be able to hunt squirrels.

Additionally, you may also need to have some type of safety certification prior to purchasing a license.

Ensure that you have the proper license and safety certification before doing any type of hunting.

Legal aspects to consider before hunting:

- Area you are hunting

- Specific hunting dates

- Safety certification

Area

When you are going to purchase your hunting license, the first thing you will need to know is what area you plan to hunt. Most small game hunting licenses are good for the entire state that you purchase the license in, but if you will be hunting in multiple states then you will probably need multiple licenses.

Be aware that if you are not a resident of the state you plan to hunt in, you will typically pay a higher rate for your license. Sometimes it can be as much as double what it costs for a resident of that state to buy a license.

You should also consider what other type of hunting or fishing you plan to do within that year before you buy a hunting license. Some states allow you to purchase a combination license that will give you hunting and fishing privileges for a discounted rate. Not only do you save money this way, it also helps reduce the amount of paperwork you need to carry with you.

Hunting Dates

Not only do you need to know what areas you plan to hunt squirrels, you will also need to know the dates you plan to hunt them. Most states' small game hunting licenses are good for a season, usually September through December.

Just be sure you understand the regulations to ensure that you are covered during the dates that you plan to hunt. Unfortunately, not knowing the rules is not a valid excuse if a game warden catches you without proper licensing. The penalties can be very harsh for people who violate the rules including loss of hunting privileges and confiscation of hunting equipment.

Safety Certification

In addition to having proper licensing, you will also need to ensure that you obtain any necessary safety certifications prior to hunting squirrels. Again, the rules in each area are different. In some areas you will need to have a formal safety certification regardless of your age. In other areas if you are over a certain age you do not need to have safety training.

Even if your area does not require any safety training, it is an excellent idea to go through a safety training course prior to doing any type of hunting. Although hunting can be a very fun activity, it also comes with a certain level of safety risk.

You can never eliminate all safety risks when hunting, but going through a formal safety class will teach you the skills to improve your safety practices. Hunting safety courses often range from $20-$100 for a few-week-long course. This is a great investment in your long term safety.

Now let's examine gun types...

Step 3: Gun Types

Select from a Variety of Weapons for Hunting Squirrels

As with many types of hunting there is a large range of weapons to select from for hunting squirrels.

The good news with squirrel hunting weapons is that they are all relatively affordable. A gun used for squirrel hunting can start as low as $100 brand new. Of course you could spend a lot more if you went with the higher end brands or got a lot of extra features, but if you are just getting started in the sport and/or want to see if you enjoy the sport before you invest too much in it, there is absolutely no need to let the cost of a gun prohibit you from squirrel hunting.

Although there are other weapons to use for hunting squirrel, we are going to cover the 4 most common types of guns used for this.

Guns for squirrel hunting:

- .22 Caliber Rifle

- .17 Caliber Rifle

- Air Rifle

- Shotgun

.22 Caliber Rifle

By far the most common gun associated with hunting squirrels is the .22 rifle. This rifle is a staple for all types of small game hunting including squirrels, rabbits, chipmunks, and a variety of other small animals.

There are several benefits to this gun including the price. A brand new .22 caliber rifle can start at just over $100 for a very basic entry level gun. The more options you add to the gun the more it will cost, but for starting off the cost is very reasonable.

In addition to the low cost of the gun, the ammunition is easier to find and is relatively inexpensive as well. I recently saw ammunition for a .22 rifle priced at 500 rounds for $25. This is much less expensive then ammunition for a .17 caliber rifle or a shotgun. Also, since .22 rifles are so common, it is easy to find the ammunition. Even stores such as Wal-Mart will carry ammunition for your .22 caliber rifle.

The final benefit of the .22 caliber rifle is the penetration size of the bullets. These bullets are very lethal when you shoot a squirrel, but are small enough that with a properly-placed shot they do not waste much meat. Especially with a headshot you will not lose any meat. If you compare this to a bullet from a larger caliber rifle or even a shotgun, this bullet is much smaller and will therefore allow you to have access to more of the meat.

.22 caliber rifles will come in a variety of reloading action styles. The first type is a bolt action style meaning that you pull a lever back to load or "cock" the gun after you shoot to bring the next bullet into the chamber. Another type is a semi-auto style which is where the gun automatically reloads itself after each time it is fired. The final way these guns can be reloaded is by using a pumping action on the mid-section of the gun.

.17 Caliber Rifle

The .17 caliber rifle is similar in look to a .22 caliber rifle and many of the features will be nearly identical. Contrary to the .22 caliber rifle which has several styles for reloading, these guns mostly come in a bolt action style for reloading.

A .17 caliber rifle actually has a smaller diameter bullet than the .22 caliber which can allow a squirrel hunter to make a very accurate shot and keep the size of the bullet penetration area relatively small in order to preserve meat.

This style of rifle has become very popular for small game as a lot of hunters feel these guns are slightly more accurate than .22 caliber rifles and can have a longer distance shooting range. For the last several years I have been using the .17 caliber rifle for squirrel hunting and I have been very satisfied with this gun.

A downside of this gun is the cost of ammunition. The lowest price I have found on ammunition for these guns is about $10 for a pack of 50 rounds which is about $.20 per round. If you compare this to the .22 rifle where you can find ammunition on sale for about $.05 per round, you can see that it is clearly more expensive.

Air Rifle

Air rifles have made a huge entrance into small game hunting over the last decade or so. Contrary to the old style BB guns and pellet guns, air rifles are significantly more powerful and more accurate.

One benefit of air rifles is they are fairly lightweight and easy to handle. This makes them an excellent choice for training youth to hunt. They are powerful enough to kill a squirrel with an accurately-placed shot, but not likely to be lethal to a human. You still would not want to be shot by one of these, but they serve as a safer way to teach young hunters how to hunt.

Air rifles are usually break-barrel or CO2-operated. The break-barrel style is operated by pulling the barrel down at a hinge which is attached to a spring mechanism. After you load in your pellet you then move the barrel back into place. You can then fire the rifle and repeat the cocking action to load your next round.

The CO2-operated air rifles are powered by small canisters of CO2 inserted into the gun. You simply pull the trigger to shoot pellets that are projected by powerful bursts of air.

Another benefit of air rifles is that the ammunition is inexpensive and easy to find. You can buy the ammunition at sporting good shops and even most hardware stores. A box of a few hundred pellets is just a couple of dollars.

Shotguns

There are a wide variety of shotguns to select from to use for squirrel hunting. Two types are semi-auto and pump shotguns. Semi-auto shotguns automatically load in the next shell after you shoot, whereas pump shotguns require you to use the pump mechanism to load in the next round.

Using a shotgun to hunt squirrels is one of the best ways to ensure that you will hit your target. This is because many BBs are projected out from a single shot. Their kill radius can be 2-3 feet wide, particularly when shooting at close range.

For those hunters who are specifically hunting for the food, you should really consider hunting with a shotgun. However, if you want to have more of a challenge when you are squirrel hunting, then you should go with one of the other gun options.

Shotguns will be the most expensive of any of the guns that you can purchase for squirrel hunting. The least expensive shotguns start around $250 and can go up to several thousand dollars.

Now let's take a look at gun accessories that you may want to consider…

Step 4: Gun Accessories

What Accessories Can You Get for Your Gun?

The most obvious type of accessory that you will need for your gun is the shells, but there are many other accessories that you should consider for squirrel hunting as well.

Gun accessories to consider:

- Scopes

- Slings

- Extended Capacity Magazines

Scopes

A scope is something you put on the top of your gun to look through when aiming and is similar to binoculars in that it helps magnify distances, making far away objects appear closer, but it also gives an aiming point.

Let's look at a few pros and cons of scopes:

Pros:

- Magnify objects so they appear closer, and gives an aiming point

- Can add accuracy if the squirrel is not moving too fast

Cons:

- Cost can be anywhere from $40-500 or more

- If the squirrel is moving fast it can make it harder to aim and shoot

- Can take away the challenge of seeing your target without a scope

Having a scope is helpful for shooting squirrels at the tops of trees since they are further away. They also might be mostly hidden by the branches and leaves so this helps with the smaller area of visibility on the squirrel.

One of the downsides to a scope is when squirrels are moving fast. Scopes make it more difficult to get an accurate shot with a moving object because they magnify all of the surroundings as well as the target, making it more challenging to see the actual target. Think of a scope as being similar to binoculars. They are good for looking at objects that are still, but for objects that are moving, it can be disorienting to keep up with them.

Another reason people might not use a scope is to add a level of challenge to their hunt. I often switch between a scoped gun and an open sight gun. Both have their advantages and disadvantages so I use whichever gun I am in the mood for that day.

Slings

If you have a long walk to your hunting location a sling can be a great way to make carrying your gun easier. Basically, a sling is a strap that attaches to both ends of your gun and goes over your shoulder to free up your hands. This allows you to carry other items and makes it easier to go over some of the difficult terrain you might encounter outdoors.

Depending on the type of gun you purchase it may or may not have sling holes. Basically, a sling hole is where you attach the sling to your gun. These usually are small metal tabs on the gun that have a hole in the middle. You run the fastening bar of the sling through these holes to secure the sling. If your gun does not have these sling loops you can have a gunsmith install them for about $20.

Slings are usually inexpensive, ranging from about $10-$30.

Extended Capacity Magazines

Some guns have the option to add an extended capacity magazine. Basically, these serve the purpose of allowing you to hold more bullets in the magazine than what is possible with the standard magazine that the gun comes with.

For example, the standard capacity of a magazine for a .17 caliber gun is usually around 5-6 bullets. However, with an extended capacity magazine they could hold anywhere from 10-20 bullets, or even more. When you are taking several shots at squirrels these extended capacity magazines can be very convenient.

Now let's discuss what else you should consider bringing with you on your hunt…

Step 5: What Else to Bring Hunting

Bring these Items to Prepare for Hunting Squirrels

Now that we have discussed weapon types and gun accessories, let's take a look at some of the other items that you may want to bring with you on your hunting trip.

What else I should bring hunting:

- Hunting knife

- Compass

- Vest with game pocket

- Food & water

Hunting Knife

A hunting knife is one of the most important items that you will want to bring with you on your outdoor adventure. After you shoot a squirrel, you will need a knife to be able to clean it. You will remove the guts and skin of the squirrel and usually the best place to leave the guts is in the wood.

Make sure that you sharpen your knife before you go as a sharp knife makes cutting easier. Surprisingly a sharp knife adds to your safety because you don't have to push as hard to cut which reduces the chance of the knife slipping and cutting you.

Compass

Depending on the area you are going to hunt and how familar you are with the woods you are in, it can be a great idea to bring a compass with you. In most cases, in the areas that I hunt I know the land extremely well and don't bring a compass.

However, anytime that you are hunting a new area that you have never been to before you sould bring a compass for safety. The chances of getting lost are pretty slim, but it is best to have one with you to be safe.

As an alternative to bringing a separate compass, many smart phones now either have compasses installed on them from the factory or have compass applications available for download. This is a nice feature so you do not need to purchase or bring a separate compass.

The only downside to relying on your phone for a compass is you need to be sure that your phone is charged and that you will be an area that has cell phone service, as often these apps only work when there is cell phone reception.

Vest With Game Pocket

We discussed clothing in an earlier section, but it is worth stressing the importance of a vest with a game pocket again. These vest types are often seen on pheasant hunters but they also make them for small game hunting.

Basically, these are hunting vests that have a pouch on the back side in which you can store the game that you shoot. Ideally you will shoot several squirrels when you are hunting, so it good to have a way to carry them as you continue to hunt or while you are walking home.

Another alternative if you do not have a vest with a pocket is to consider using a backpack. I would recommend using a backpack that can be dedicated to the purpose of carrying squirrels though as you would not want to use it for anything else after this.

If you do not have a vest with a pocket or a backpack, you will have to carry the squirrel(s) you shoot by hand. This is a problem if you want to continue hunting because if you see another squirrel, you will have to lay the squirrel(s) down and then take the time to come back and find it(them) after you chase down the next squirrel. If this is your only option, then at least make sure you carry the squirrel(s) by the tail as this is the best way to carry them.

Food & Water

It is never a bad idea to bring some water and a few snacks with you on any hunting trip. When you are going for just an hour or so, a bottle of water and a snack bar should get you through. Having just this little bit of food and water can help keep you hydrated and energized.

When you plan longer trips you may want to bring a few bottles of water and even pack a lunch. "Still" hunting for squirrels can involve a few hours of sitting and waiting as you shoot squirrels. If you don't have food and water it may cause you to have to go back sooner than you want. As long as you have food and water you can extend your hunting trip, which is particularly important on those days when you are having a lot of success.

Now let's find out where to hunt...

Step 6: Where to Hunt

How to Select the Proper Location to Hunt Squirrels

Finding good hunting spots can help you improve your chances of success with squirrel hunting. Let's take a look at some places to go squirrel hunting.

Identifying areas for squirrel hunting:

- Pay attention to where you see squirrels

- Woods

- Areas near standing corn or other crops

- Near barns and corn cribs

Pay Attention to Where you See Squirrels

This should be obvious but you want to pay attention to where you see squirrels. When you are driving around, keep an eye out in the fields and woods and actively look for squirrels. If you often see squirrels in a certain area this should be a great place for you to start.

Also, you can ask your friends and family to be on the lookout for you. Let them know that you want to go squirrel hunting and ask if they could pay attention to where they are seeing them. It is better to have several people searching for squirrels rather than just you and mostly likely friends and family will be willing to help you out with this.

Another strategy to find good places to hunt is to make a posting on your favorite social media website. Post that you are looking to go squirrel hunting and ask if anybody has suggestions on where to go. This is a great way to get the word out to a lot of people at once and quite often people will be willing to help you out and provide some ideas.

Woods

The majority of hunting for squirrels is done in the woods. This is because squirrels use the tall trees as a place to build their nests. The sticks and leaves provide quick building resources for their nests. Also, by having their nests high up in the air, it provides them the ability to see predators coming from a distance.

Squirrels also use the trees as a hiding spot. They go into hollowed out cavities of trees as a very fast and effective way to get away from humans and other predators.

When you go searching for squirrels in the woods the most common place you will see them is in the trees. What I like to do when I am looking for a place to hunt squirrels is stand in the woods and just be still for a few minutes and scan the tops of trees. It usually does not take long before you see some squirrel movement.

When squirrels jump from one tree to the next you can often see the branches shake back and forth quite a bit. When you see movement in the trees, squirrels are the most likely culprit.

Areas Near Standing Corn or Other Crops

Similar to many animals, squirrels like easy-to-find food sources, so they will often nest near a field that has crops, such as corn. Corn fields provide squirrels a great food resource for several months out of the year as the corn grows and even after the corn is harvested. Woods that are next to a field with crops in it can be one of the very best places to find squirrels.

Near Barns and Corn Cribs

If given the choice, squirrels really prefer when they don't even need to go to a field for food. Many crop farmers use some type of silo or corn crib to hold their corn and crops and this is truly a squirrel's dream. An open corn crib could feed a group of squirrels for months.

When I go hunting one of the first places I check is near these corn cribs because there is usually at least one squirrel in or on top of the crib. If there is not one on it then there is usually one very close by.

As far as squirrels go, if you find their food source then you are more than likely to find some squirrels.

Now let's discuss how to get permission to hunt private land...

Step 7: How to Get Permission to Hunt Private Land

Tips for Non-Landowners

If you are like me, you do not own hunting land and do not want to battle other hunters for public land. If this is your situation then you will need to get permission to hunt private land.

At first it can feel a little uncomfortable to ask other people to use their land for hunting, however, after some experience the process gets much easier. Also, if you get permission to hunt on someone's land one time, they are pretty likely to let you come back again in the future.

How to get permission to hunt private land:

- Don't be afraid to ask

- Don't wear hunting clothes when approaching them to ask

- Be kind and smile

- Bring a youth hunter if possible

- Tell them exact times you will be there

- Do a favor in return

- Bring them meat or another gift

- Thank them after

Don't Be Afraid to Ask

Something that holds hunters back from finding land to hunt is the fear of asking for permission. People can feel intimidated by asking landowners for permission to hunt on their property and I shared the same fear when I first hunting, but the more you do it the more you get used to it.

When you are turned down, the primary reason is that they already have a friend or family member that hunts the area. I have never had anyone get upset at me for asking.

Sample Wording to Use When Asking Permission:

- Hello, my name is ___ and I am hoping to do some squirrel hunting tomorrow. It seems like you have a great piece of land for squirrel hunting. Would it be okay with you if I hunted on your property this weekend?

- Good afternoon, I am looking for a place to squirrel hunt with my daughter tomorrow. Would it be possible for us to hunt on your land for squirrel for a few hours in the afternoon?

- Hello, I was driving by and I saw several squirrels in your trees. I really enjoy squirrel hunting and I'm wondering if it would be okay with you if I could hunt here for a few hours today.

If they say no, don't waste this opportunity to find a hunting spot. Say "Thank you, I understand. Do you happen to know of any other places nearby that you would suggest that I try?" They might know another landowner that would allow you to hunt nearby or they might know of some good public land for hunting in the area.

Don't Wear Hunting Clothing

I recommend not wearing hunting clothing when you go to ask for permission to hunt on someone's property because it can give the landowners a feeling that you are assuming that you will be able to hunt there. Not all people like or allow hunting so don't assume anything.

If you are planning on hunting that same day, at least take off your orange hat and hunting vest. It should not take too much to remove the items that make you look like a hunter. If you are dressed like you are ready to hunt, it can also give them the impression that you may go hunt on their land even if they do not give you permission.

Be Kind and Smile

This should go without saying but if you are polite to the landowner they will more than likely be polite back. Be conscious when you approach the property to put a smile on your face to ensure that you are received as a friendly individual.

Be sure to make the impression that you are friendly and easy to get along with. Do what you can to strike up a conversation with the landowner by asking them some questions such as how long they have lived at the property and what they do for a living. People love to talk about themselves so if you can get the conversation going and let the landowner talk, it will likely improve your chances of getting permission to hunt their land.

If they do agree to allow you to hunt on their property, keep the conversation going and ask them where on their property in particular they would recommend hunting. After all, they should know best where the squirrels will be on their property.

Bring a Youth Hunter

Most people have a soft spot for children and if you are planning on hunting with a child it can help to bring them with you when you ask for permission. People who would have said no to you alone may say yes if it means that a child will get the opportunity to experience the outdoors.

Another benefit of bringing a child is that it can be a great learning experience for them. This helps get the child used to speaking to strangers and helps them learn all of the aspects of hunting that will be valuable to them when they start hunting on their own.

Tell Them the Exact Times You Will Be There

To help put the landowners at ease, it is important to let them know exactly when you plan to hunt. If you want to hunt just one morning, tell them that. Or if you want access for an entire weekend, be specific so they are not taken off guard when they see you on their property.

This is very important because people will feel more comfortable knowing the exact times that they can expect to see you rather than having you show up at any random time of the day.

Never go hunting on someone else's property at a time when you do not have permission.

Do a Favor In Return

Landowners often have work that needs to be done around their property, particularly if they are farmers. Ask them if there are a few projects that you could help out with for an afternoon or two in exchange for hunting on their property.

Not only would assisting with these chores be a way to get permission to hunt, it is also a great way to form a relationship with the landowner. The more you get to know them, the more likely they are to let you to continue to hunt there.

Bring them Meat or Other Small Gifts

Another thing you can ask is if the landowners would like to have some meat in exchange for allowing you to hunt there. Even if they don't hunt, most people may like getting some free meat. This can be a great win-win situation for both parties.

Not all people like squirrel meat so you could bring some other type of small gift as a way to say thank you to the landowner for allowing you to use their property. You could bake some cookies in advance or stop at the store on the way and buy some cookies to give them.

It does not have to be anything very expensive but something simple can go a long way in letting them know that you appreciate their generosity in allowing you to hunt on their property.

Benefits of Getting Permission Effectively

If you follow these steps and are respectful with those who allow you to hunt their land, you may end up with one or more long term hunting spot(s). Be kind when asking, do something in return, and get to know the landowners. The better connections you make with people, the more likely you will build a great network and have multiple hunting locations that you can use.

Our next section covers finding public land for squirrel hunting…

Step 8: Finding Public Land to Hunt

Public Land Can Provide Excellent Hunting Opportunities

Similar to private land, with a little effort you can find some great hunting spots available on public land.

Types of public land available for hunting:

- WMAs or Wildlife Management Areas

- State Forests

- Wildlife Refuges

- National Forests

- County Land

- and many more...

Tips about using public land:

- Search online

- Contact your state wildlife office

- Scout the area in advance

- Be safe

Search Online

With a little online research you will be sure to find some public hunting land within a reasonable driving distance from your home. Simply search online using any of the terms listed above under "Types of public land available for hunting" followed by your state or county name and there will be a listing.

Each state has different regulations for these areas so if you have questions regarding hunting regulations that are not clearly outlined online, be sure to reach out to your state wildlife office directly.

Contact Your State Wildlife Office

State wildlife officers are usually very friendly people and passionate about the outdoors. Don't be afraid to call the wildlife office and ask them what areas they would suggest nearby for you to try squirrel hunting. They want to help people enjoy the outdoors so if you ask, they are going to be happy to assist.

Scout the Area in Advance

Once you have a site in mind, if possible it is great to scout the area in advance. Try driving to the hunting location a few days prior to actually hunting and review the territory. You can do this by taking a walk through the woods and making note of where you see squirrels.

Even if you are unable to physically go to the hunting spot in advance, you can use online resources to help you plan your hunt. Since you may have found this location by looking online for public hunting areas, you can usually find online maps for these public lands as well.

Scan those maps to see where the woods are located as well as nearby fields, etc. This will help you plan your walking path in advance and hopefully help you improve your chances of success.

Safety

Safety is the primary thing to be aware of when hunting on public land. Since it is public land, anyone can use this land and there is no way to guarantee that you are alone in the woods.

You need to ensure that you are wearing proper hunting attire that we discussed earlier. In most cases this means wearing blaze orange on the top half of your body. By doing this it will allow other hunters to see you more easily.

Additionally, it is important to check your surroundings before you shoot. It is easy to get caught up in the excitement of shooting and forget what is around you. You want to think about what is in the direction you are shooting as bullets can travel a long distance. You need to be 100% sure that there is nobody in the vicinity that could possibly get hit.

If you are ever in doubt if you have a safe shot, do not shoot.

Now let's discuss how you can prepare for your hunt...

Step 9: Prepping for Your Hunt

A Little Prep Time Goes a Long Way for a Successful Hunt

Before you head out for your hunt, ensure you are fully prepared for a fun outdoor adventure.

What you should do to prepare for your hunt:

- Inspect all equipment & guns

- Purchase ammunition & licenses

- Have a checklist of items to bring

Inspect all Equipment & Guns

It is very important to inspect all of your hunting equipment including your guns before going out hunting. Sharpen your hunting knives and make sure all of your clothes are in good condition.

Also make sure your guns are in proper working order. If you are hunting with a scope you should test the gun each year to ensure that the scope is still sighted in. With any gun it is a good idea to shoot a few rounds prior to the hunting season to ensure everything is in working order and it is shooting accurately.

Proper gun care involves thoroughly cleaning your guns before you go hunting for the first time each season, as well as a few times throughout the season, and again before you put them away for the year. So even though I cleaned my gun at the end of the previous season, I will be sure to also clean it as again I get everything ready for the next season in case any dust or other items settled on my gun during storage.

One of the best cleaning tools that I have come across is called a bore snake and it is made to clean out the barrel of your gun. They typically cost about $20 and are very easy to use. Bore snakes are about 10 inches long and have a 20 inch rope with a metal piece on one end that you drop into one end of your barrel. The rope comes out the other end of the barrel and you simply grab it and pull the entire unit through your barrel.

As the bore snake moves through your barrel there are tiny bristles and fabric that help collect and clean out any dirt and gunpowder residue. You simply run the bore snake through your barrel 2 or 3 times and it is clean. This is much faster than using a rod with cleaning swaps attached to the end.

Purchase Ammunition & Licenses

You will want to ensure you have all of your licenses purchased in advance. We discussed licenses earlier but it is worth mentioning again to avoid any illegal hunting. Additionally, there are often cut off dates for buying licenses. Even if there are not cut off dates, many areas have a waiting period where it takes 1-2 days for a purchased license to become effective. This is to prevent people from shooting a squirrel and then going directly to a store to buy the license.

Having ammunition on hand is also important. The good thing about ammunition is it really does not expire, at least not for many years. For people who hunt in remote areas it is even more important to have enough ammunition because you cannot easily get to a store to purchase more. Err on the side of having extra ammunition as you can always save the leftover to use later.

Checklist of Items to Bring

Taking a little time to create a checklist of all of the items you will need on your hunting trip is a great way to ensure that you are prepared for an enjoyable hunt. Before you leave on your hunting trip, double-check your list to make sure nothing is missed.

Do you have your ammunition? Do you have a compass? Do you have your knife? All of these are critical items to ensure that you are ready for a fun day of squirrel hunting. I can tell you from experience that it will quickly put a damper on your hunting trip if you forget one of these critical items.

One time I forgot the magazine to hold the bullets for my gun. I realized this after I had already driven a half hour to my hunting spot. It was so frustrating to have spent so much time getting prepared and driving to the spot and then realizing I forgot something so simple. Do yourself a favor and create a basic checklist to ensure this does not happen to you.

Now let's look at the different seasons for squirrel hunting...

Step 10: Hunting Seasons

Enjoy the Challenges and Opportunities Created By Each Season

Every season provides unique opportunities for hunting squirrels. This is one thing that keeps this sport fun and exciting as no matter what time of year you go, you will find new opportunities and challenges to overcome. Let's take a look at the seasons for squirrel hunting and what they provide as far as hunting excitement.

Seasons:

- Early Season

- Mid-Season

- Late Season

Early Season

Typically the early season includes late August and early September. One clear benefit of hunting during the early season is the temperature. Regardless of where you are located, this time of year you will usually experience warm to moderate temperatures.

If you are doing "still" hunting this will be ideal, however if you are doing active hunting it could get a little warm.

After going 6 months or more without hunting, it can be so exciting to rush out to the woods and hunt on opening day of squirrel season.

However, the early season will present a huge challenge in regards to visibility of squirrels. Leaves, brush, and more will still all be on the trees and ground and these will create difficult hunting situations. During this time of year a squirrel on a tree full of leaves will be challenging to see, much less shoot successfully.

Mid-Season

As the year progresses it becomes easier to see squirrels in the trees and on the ground. Late September and the month of October are when the majority of leaves fall off trees. In addition, the shrubs and brush on the ground will thin out which will help create more clear visibility of squirrels.

To be successful in hunting squirrels you need to be able to see them, so the mid-season is often the best time of year to shoot squirrels. Pinning a squirrel down on the side of a tree without any leaves is one of the easiest shooting opportunities that you will ever get.

Another benefit of the mid-season is that the temperatures are cool enough but not too cold where you will be uncomfortable for hunting. Having cooler temperatures is especially nice if you plan to "active" hunt squirrels where you move through the woods at a quick pace.

Late Season

The late season is usually November and December and will present significantly lower temperatures. In addition to the lower temperatures, you may also have to deal with snow.

To deal with these temperatures ensure that you dress appropriately with a thicker coat and winter boots. You may need to step up your apparel even further if you are going to do "still" hunting for squirrels.

During this time of year you will have the benefit of very clear trees and even cleared ground to see squirrels. There should be very little leaves left on trees at this point and most of the vegetation at ground level will have significantly cleared out as well.

Tracking is another benefit of hunting in the late season when there is snow on the ground. Snow makes it very easy to see tracks on the ground. You can follow these tracks to find the squirrels.

Step 11: Time of Day for Squirrel Hunting

Use Squirrel Behavior to Your Benefit

The good news is that squirrels can be hunted pretty much any time of day, so don't be discouraged if you cannot get out hunting in the first half hour of daylight.

In this section we will discuss the times of day and how each can be effective for squirrel hunting.

Times to hunt squirrels:

- Morning

- Afternoon

- Evening

- Squirrel hunting as a time filler for other hunting

Morning

Taking advantage of the morning feeding time is an excellent way to bag some squirrel. As the sun comes up in the morning the squirrels begin to get off their resting spots and nests to head out to feed.

If you are set up in your squirrel hunting spot first thing in the morning the chances are that you will get some excellent hunting opportunities.

Afternoon

It is possible to have squirrel hunting success during the entire day. In fact, some of my best squirrel hunting trips have been in the afternoon.

The afternoons have great visibility due to the sun being higher in the sky so you can pick out the squirrels easier. You also get to enjoy the warmer temperatures of the afternoon compared to cooler temperatures in the morning and evening.

Evening

Evening hunting includes the last hour or two of sunlight. Check your local regulations to see how late into the evening you can hunt legally. Similar to the morning, squirrels come out during this time to feed.

Since squirrels will be feeding they will be out in the trees which should give you a good chance of seeing one and hopefully shooting it.

Squirrel Hunting as a Filler for Other Hunting

Tracking through the woods for squirrels is a great way to pass some extra time when you are hunting for other animals.

For example, I hunt for ducks and geese and the prime time for them is the first few hours of the morning. So after we get our fill of ducks and geese and before we are ready to leave the woods for the day, we grab our squirrel rifles and take a half hour to walk the area for squirrels.

I really enjoy the extra variety that it adds to my day. Additionally, it helps extend the hunting day as the ducks and geese in my area are very hard to come by after about 10am.

The other thing I commonly do is incorporate squirrel hunting with other small game hunting at the exact same time. Other small game such as rabbits, chipmunks, grouse and pheasants are all found in the same type of environments as squirrels. If you pay attention and get the proper licensing for all of these animals, it is possible that you could come home with a nice mixed bag of small game that you harvested all in one trip.

Now we will take a look at how to identify squirrels…

Step 12: Identifying Squirrels

Learn the Various Types of Squirrels Before Hunting

It is extremely important to know what type of squirrel you are shooting at before you pull the trigger. Depending on your area and the license you purchased you may only be able to shoot certain types of squirrels.

Types of squirrel:

- Grey Squirrels
- Fox Squirrels
- Red Squirrels
- Flying Squirrels

Grey Squirrels

Grey squirrels are found throughout the majority of the United States and are one of the largest species of squirrels. Although they are called grey squirrels, they actually come in a variety of colors, which include black, gray, brown, cream and red.

These are pretty good sized squirrels with their bodies being about 1 foot long and their tail adding another 6-8 inches to their overall length. The grey squirrels can get up to about 1 to 1 ½ pounds in weight.

Another interesting fact about these squirrels is that they will bury food when there is an abundance of a food source to save it for a later date. Often squirrels will do this in the summer and fall to prepare for the winter months when the food sources will be more limited. They have a very good sense of memory when it comes to relocating their buried food.

Fox Squirrels

Compared to grey squirrels, fox squirrels are some of the larger squirrels you will find usually ranging from 17 inches to 27 inches. They can weigh anywhere from 1 pound up to about 2 ½ pounds making them even larger than the common grey squirrel.

These squirrels usually have a dark fur color such as black or tan and their underside is a gold, reddish or orange. You may also notice that fox squirrels are very vocal, meaning that they make a lot of different noises to communicate with other squirrels in the area.

Fox squirrels are often found in oak, walnut, pine and hickory trees which all are good sources of the nuts that they enjoy feasting on.

Red Squirrels

Red squirrels are one of the smaller varieties of squirrels that you will encounter. They are about half the size of the fox squirrel. Their bodies are about 7-9 inches in length, but what you might notice is how long their tail is. Red squirrels' tails can be up 15 inches long, meaning that their tail is actually longer then their body. The weight of these squirrels is about 1 pound to 1 ½ pounds.

As their name indicates, they are red in color. Their color is a rusty red color and if you find them in oak trees they are easier to pick out than other squirrels due to their color.

Another interesting fact about the red squirrel is that it sheds its fur two times per year. One time it sheds its fur to go to a lighter fur in preparation for the warm summer months, and the second time it sheds as the winter approaches to switch over to a heavier coat for warmth.

Flying Squirrels

Flying squirrels are usually found in the higher elevation states and are one of the most unique types of squirrels. These squirrels have long flaps of skin that almost look like wings between their legs that act as gliding mechanisms.

The flying squirrels use these to glide from tree to tree. They are small in size from about 7-9 inches long and weigh just a few ounces. The flying squirrels usually come out at night so they are a challenging squirrel to be able to shoot as you typically cannot hunt for squirrels in the evening.

Now let's examine how to find signs of squirrels...

Step 13: Looking for Signs of Squirrels

Pay Attention to Locate Squirrels

A key to successfully hunting for squirrels is to try to find a place with signs of squirrels in the area. If you find some of these signs then it is likely that you will be able to find squirrels nearby.

Common signs of squirrels in the area:

- Footprints
- Droppings (i.e. poop)
- Squirrel nests in trees
- Sounds of squirrels communicating

Footprints

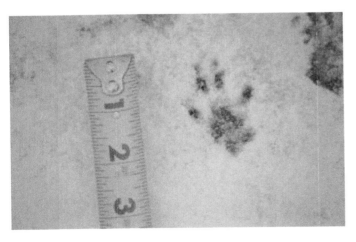

One way to know that squirrels are in the area is by the footprints they leave behind. However, depending on the time of year that you are hunting it can be challenging to find squirrel footprints because they often run in the trees. Also, when they do run on the ground there is not always mud or snow to leave their tracks behind.

Hunting for squirrels in the snow will be one of the best times to be able to see where squirrels are traveling from the footprints they leave behind. Their footprints are very small, just a few inches long. Their front paws are about 1 inch long and ¾ inch wide. Rear paws will be slightly longer at 1 ¼ inches long and close to an inch wide.

Droppings

Another indicator of squirrels in the area is their droppings. Squirrel droppings are about 1 inch long, black and in the shape of a small cylinder. You will usually see a pile of these in one place. Typically a pile of about 5-10 or more is what you will see.

As you walk through the woods be sure to take time not only look in the trees but also look down for droppings on the ground. If you do find a pile of droppings you should stop to examine them for a moment.

If you look at the droppings and they have a wet appearance than that means that the droppings are fresh and that the squirrels were in the area recently. When the droppings have a dried out appearance that means they are old and the squirrels might have moved on from this spot.

It might feel odd to be examining poop, but I find the technique very useful as it helps me determine whether I should stay in a particular area to hunt for squirrels. If there is fresh poop I will be motivated to stick around as there is a good chance that a squirrel is in the area. However, if the droppings are older I am more apt to move on to the next hunting spot.

Squirrel Nests in Trees

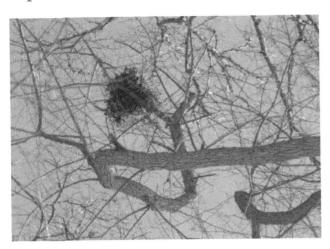

Squirrel nests are one of the easiest-to-find signs of squirrels as their nests are large and towards the top or middle of the trees. They usually make their nests out of leaves and branches that they have found in nearby areas.

The nests basically look like a ball of leaves on a branch of a tree or in the "Y" of two tree branches that are joined together. If the squirrel is in the nest you will most likely not be able to see the squirrel because of the leaves and branches, but if you sit nearby an area where there is a nest then your chances of a squirrel eventually leaving the nest or coming to the nest are pretty good.

Sound of Squirrels Communicating

As you walk through the woods you may hear the squirrels communicating with each other and they might actually communicate with you.

The reason that they would communicate with you is to try to scare you off and to show that they are agitated that you are in the area. They make a rapid "tick" sound with their teeth that can be very loud, especially in quiet woods.

The squirrels might also communicate with one another before they notice that you are approaching their area. Once you start to learn the sound of squirrels, you can use this to your advantage to find them quickly in the woods.

Step 14: Squirrel Hunting with the "Still" Method

Enjoy The Outdoors As you Wait For Squirrels

One way to partake in squirrel hunting is the "still" method which means that you sit and wait for squirrels to come into range for you to shoot them.

In my opinion, this is one of the most relaxing ways to hunt because you get to take some time and just be a part of nature while you wait.

Strategies for "still" hunting

- Identify high traffic areas
- Find a good spot to sit
- Continually scan the woods
- Listen closely for squirrels

Identify High Traffic Areas

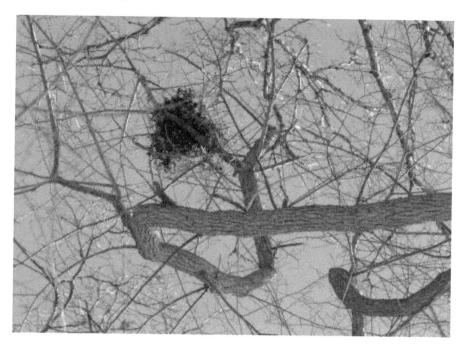

Earlier we discussed how to identify signs of squirrels. In order to have hunting success by "still" hunting you will want to put those skills to use. Look for areas where you see a lot of squirrel tracks, nests and droppings. Once you have identified such an area you are much more likely to find squirrels.

For "still" hunting I want to emphasize that taking time to find the high traffic areas is very important to be successful with this technique. If you have found a spot with a lot of good signs of squirrels, the chances of having squirrels come to you are pretty high because it is likely there are squirrels in the area. However, if you set up in an area where there is no sign of squirrels then you could sit all day without any luck.

Find a Good Spot to Sit

After finding a high traffic area it is time to find a good spot to sit. A few things to keep in mind when you are looking for a spot to sit are how far you are able to see from that spot, how much cover the spot provides you from being seen by squirrels, and how high you will be sitting off of the ground.

Some common spots to sit are: on the ground leaning up against a tree trunk; on top of a log; and on a large rock. Sitting on a large rock or a log can provide you a little extra elevation that will help you see further, however, sitting against the trunk of a tree provides excellent stability when you are ready to shoot at squirrels.

You should pay attention to how well you are blocked from the sight of squirrels where you are sitting. Finding a spot that has some brush in front of you that will hide your movement is good. Of course you still need to be able to see and have a good shot, so don't sit where the branches or tall grass inhibit your ability to point your gun and shoot at the squirrels.

Continually Scan the Woods

Sometimes squirrels are very easy to see and other times they can be a little more challenging to find. The easiest time to see squirrels is when they are running through trees. They can jump from one tree to the next as they move through the woods.

As they jump from tree to tree the branches will shake and it will be nearly impossible to miss seeing them. In addition to the movement this creates, it also creates a good amount of noise, so if you don't see them right away you will at least hear them.

While you sit in place you want to continuously look back and forth throughout the woods for any sign of movement. Again, tree tops are good places to look for squirrels but they often run along the ground as well.

Start with your head facing as far left as possible and then slowly move your head to the right. Look up and down as you move your head left to right. Once you are looking as far right as possible, slowly move your head back to the left. Continue this back and forth scanning until you find a squirrel.

Listen Closely For Squirrels

You will notice that as you walk through the woods to find a good spot to hunt that the woods may seem loud. This is because of the sound you are making by rustling through leaves and breaking branches as you walk.

However, once you stop and sit down you will notice that within just a minute or two the sound of the woods will become very quiet and you will start to hear small movements in your area.

When squirrels walk along the ground they are actually very noisy. In fact, they often sound like deer or other large animals due to the amount of noise they make. I find it quite amazing how much noise a small squirrel can produce.

When they walk on the ground they will usually run or walk for a few moments and then stop briefly. After stopping they will pick back up and keep moving along. If you think you hear a squirrel but then the sounds stops that is normal. Now is the time to use sight along with your sense of hearing to find squirrels. Move your eyes to the direction that you heard the noise and wait a few moments to see if they start moving again.

As we discussed earlier you might also hear the squirrels in the trees. When squirrels jump from one tree to the next they make a good amount of sound and movement so you should be able to easily hear if a squirrel is traveling through the trees nearby.

Now let's take a look at how to stalk squirrels…

Step 15: Stalking Squirrels

Actively Walking to Find Squirrels Can Produce Great Results

Stalking for squirrels means that you walk through the woods to actively find squirrels rather than "still" hunting and waiting for squirrels to come within range

Critical components to squirrel stalking:

- Plan your route
- Walk quietly
- Stop often and observe
- Always be ready to shoot
- Move quickly when you see squirrels in the distance

Plan Your Route

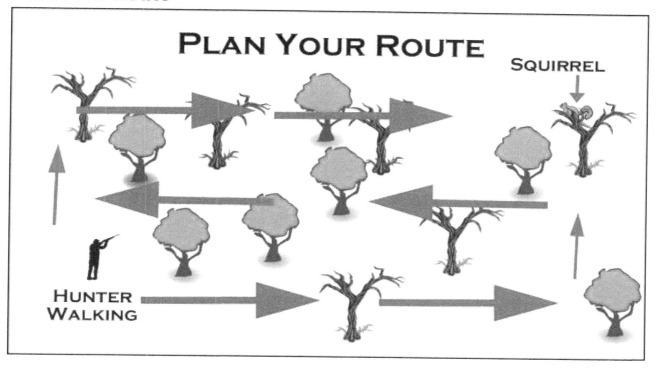

As you get ready to actively hunt for squirrels it is important to plan your route. You should think about the area you are going to be hunting and try to strategize what the best way will be to cover all of the area in the most effective manner.

If it is a small wooded area maybe you walk down half of the woods and when you get to one end you turn around and walk back down the other half of the woods.

Maybe you are hunting in a larger wooded area. Then you could try to zig-zag through the woods and eventually get from one side of the woods to the other.

You should also think about what the high traffic areas will likely be for squirrels. Areas near fields and other food sources are places that you should be sure to check. Additionally, areas near water can be fruitful as the squirrels will eventually need to drink water.

Walk Quietly

As you actively hunt for squirrel it is best to try to walk as quietly as possible. You will want to lift your feet up completely off the ground with each step and take large steps. As you set your foot back down, let your heel make contact with the ground first and then gently allow the rest of your foot down.

It is inevitable that you will make some noise as there will be branches and dry leaves that you cannot avoid stepping on, but by consciously walking quietly you will greatly reduce the amount of noise you make.

At some point the squirrels will usually hear you as you get close to them, but this can work to your advantage. Try to get close enough to the tree that they are in and then stop. If you stop and stand still the squirrel can then get confused about where you are and freeze. This provides an excellent opportunity to shoot it.

Stop Often and Observe

To ensure you have the best chance of seeing and hearing squirrels you will want to stop every 5-10 steps and actively look around. When you are walking it is hard to hear squirrels because of the amount of noise you make while walking, but when you stop it should get much quieter.

Listen closely for anything that may sound like a squirrel. You can often hear them walking through the woods as they step on leaves and as they crack branches that they step on.

In addition to listening, you should also scan your surroundings. If you see movement, watch that area closely to see if it was a squirrel. They like to walk for several feet and then stop and look around. Be sure you give it a few moments if you think you saw a squirrel because they will usually resume moving again shortly.

Always be Ready to Shoot

When walking through the woods you should keep your gun in a position that allows you to quickly get into shooting position. Have one hand on the stock near the trigger and the other hand near the base of the barrel where you normally hold your gun when shooting.

By using this technique you will be able to get the gun right up to your shoulder quickly to aim and take your shot. With squirrels, they will typically not sit in one spot for a long time so you need to be able to take these quick shots in order to be successful.

However, be careful about safety when you are walking with a loaded gun. Always be sure to keep the barrel pointed away from any other hunters and yourself. When you are traveling over logs and other difficult terrain you need to further increase your safety awareness.

Move Quickly When You See Squirrels in the Distance

When I see squirrels off in the distance I will move as quickly as possible to get close to where they are. Squirrels can move very fast through the branches of the trees so if you do not get to where they are quickly then you will likely lose out on the opportunity to shoot them.

Again, it is important to keep safety in mind as you move through the woods quickly. You want to ensure that your gun is on safe, but just in case you happen to trip that, you want to make sure the gun is not pointed in the direction of another hunter, yourself or any buildings.

You also want to be aware of any tripping hazards such as downed branches or fences. Of course if you are hunting an area you are very familiar with you should have a good idea of where the fences are, but a tree could have always fallen down in the path since the last time that you were hunting the area.

Now let's discuss party hunting for squirrels…

Step 16: Party Hunting for Squirrels

Bringing a Friend or Two Can Produce Excellent Results

"Party" hunting for squirrels refers to more than one hunter pursuing squirrels. With this method, even if bringing other hunters with you does not improve your hunting success, you can use this opportunity to enjoy spending time with friends or relatives.

However, you will find that outside of enjoying the outdoors with friends or family, having a few other hunting partners is a great way to improve your chances of bagging some squirrels.

Benefits of party hunting:

- Good for circling squirrels
- Shared bag limits
- Company

One thing that you will quickly notice about squirrels is their elusiveness. For example, when you walk up to a tree that a squirrel is climbing, the squirrel will move to the other side when you get close. This is a very smart move by the squirrel because you cannot see them when they are on the opposite side of the tree from you.

When you attempt to circle the tree to get on the same side as them, they keep moving to get away from you. They always try to stay on the opposite side of the tree from you. These surprisingly smart squirrels do this to remain hidden from you.

Of course this can present a significant challenge if you are hunting by yourself. This does not mean that you will never have success alone because there will be times when squirrels don't do this or when there is not much cover on the trees, but when you have a squirrel pinned in one tree and he is not giving you an open shot, then having another person with you is a great way to bag the squirrel.

Elements of "circling a squirrel":

- Both hunters start on one side of a tree
- One hunter stays in place
- The other hunter walks to the other side of the tree
- As the squirrel moves, the hunter with the clearest opening shoots

Both Hunters Start on One Side of a Tree

Many times when you are walking through the woods with a hunting partner you will walk parallel to each other. This is an effective technique because it allows you as a team to cover more ground together. If you keep about 10-20 yards in between you as you walk, you will be able to cover ground but also not let squirrels slip between the two of you.

Once one of the hunters sees a squirrel in a tree they should let the other hunter know. Now the other hunter should come over to assist with the hunt. The hunter who saw the squirrel should point out what tree they saw the squirrel in and approximately where the squirrel was.

One Hunter Stays in Place

After the hunters have communicated about the location of the squirrel, one of the hunters will be designated to stay in place. My recommendation is to have the hunter who initially saw the squirrel be the one who stays in place because they have the best idea of where the squirrel was last and can keep an eye on that area as the other hunter walks around the tree. They can also direct the other hunter where to go.

The hunter who stays behind should try to be very still. What this does is trick the squirrel into thinking there is now only one hunter and as the other hunter walks around the tree the squirrel will hopefully become visible to the standing hunter.

The Other Hunter Walks to the Other Side of the Tree

The second hunter walking to the other side of the tree should walk slowly around the tree and as they walk they should look up and down the tree to try to see where the squirrel is.

What typically happens is that as this hunter starts to walk around the tree the squirrel will start circling around the tree as they want to stay out of the walking hunter's visibility. This is exactly what you want to have happen.

As the Squirrel Moves, the Hunter with the Clearest Opening Shoots

Now that one hunter is walking around the tree the standing hunter will likely get a shooting opportunity soon. As the walking hunter moves to the other side of the tree the squirrel will either be forced to keep circling the tree, stay in place, or jump to the next tree.

The hope is that the squirrel will remain in the tree and either stay in place or circle the tree. The standing hunter needs to keep their eye on the tree and as soon as the squirrel becomes visible that is when they should take the shot.

Sometimes the squirrel might stay in place and that is perfectly fine because if it does stay in place then the hunter who is walking to the other side should be able to get a good shot.

Keep in mind that this is the best case scenario. Sometimes when the walking hunter circles the tree the squirrel will take off and start jumping from tree to tree to try to get away. However, if there are no other trees close enough for them to jump to, you will most likely be successful with this method.

Please keep in mind when you are using this "party" method for hunting squirrels that you want to make sure the other hunter is out of the way when you take a shot!

Now let's talk about calling for squirrels...

Step 17: Squirrel Calling

How to Get Squirrels to Come to You

Many people don't realize that there are actually some techniques that you can use to get squirrels to come to you.

Squirrel calling can be one of the most effective ways to get squirrels to come out into shooting range.

Calling

Contrary to calling for other types of animals such as ducks or geese, squirrel calling is extremely simple to learn and even your first time can be successful.

To do this you use a device called a "squirrel call." Most squirrel calls are handheld devices about 6 inches long. The base of them is usually made of plastic or wood and the top is typically made of rubber that looks like a round bulb.

To operate a squirrel call you simply hold the base of the call in one hand while you use the palm of your other hand to pump the rubber bulb. Each pump of the bulb it will make a "chirp" sound.

Changing how tightly you hold the base will change the pitch that the call makes. This is because the tighter you hold the base the more backpressure it creates. Using this call, especially at different pitches, will draw the squirrels toward the sound which they think is other squirrels.

These squirrel calls are very easy to use and are relatively inexpensive, around $10-$20.

Now let's identify effective shooting techniques...

Step 18: Shooting

A Squirrel Has Stopped and is in Sight, Now What?

When you finally have a squirrel stop on the side of a tree or on the ground, it is one of those moments that makes your heart race. This moment will be brief so you need to quickly take action to bag the squirrel.

Use these tips to make the most out of your shooting opportunities.

Shooting tips:

- Practice shooting before the hunting season
- Be patient
- Select a clear shooting lane
- Wait for the squirrel to stop
- Shot placement
- Improving shot accuracy
- Learn from missed shots

Practice Shooting Before the Hunting Season

If you have never been squirrel hunting or if you are having difficulty hitting squirrels then it might be a good idea to get some target practice before your next hunting trip. If you do not have your own land, one of the easiest and most cost effective ways to practice shooting is to visit a firing range.

Chances are you live within a half hour of a firing range where you can pay a fee to practice shooting. This is usually inexpensive as you can buy a time slot, usually in hour or half hour increments, for less than $20. This minimal investment could greatly improve your success on your next hunting trip.

Be Patient

It is so important to be patient when you are hunting for squirrels. The temptation to shoot right away when you see a squirrel is so strong but you must hold back until the squirrel slows down to a reasonable rate or stops altogether.

Unless you are hunting with a shotgun, the chance of hitting a squirrel that is running through the trees or on the ground is very slim, even for the most experienced hunters. In most cases you need to give the squirrel a chance to stop.

Sometimes they head directly to their nest or to a hole in a tree to hide when you get close. However, many times they run for a while and then stop somewhere on the tree. They typically think you cannot see them but more than likely you will be able to see some part of the squirrel in the tree.

Again, as tempting as it might be to shoot right away, it is so critical to be patient and hold tight until you have a higher percentage shot. If not, you will end up wasting a lot of ammunition and scaring off many squirrels that you would have eventually had a better shot at if you waited a little longer.

Select a Clear Shooting Lane

Waiting for a clear shooting lane goes hand in hand with being patient. You want to try to get into a position where you can see the squirrel and not have a lot of leaves or branches in the way.

This is easy to say but in reality it is difficult, especially if you are hunting in the early season. Most of the leaves are still on the trees at this time and it will be rare to have a fully clear shot. This is where some skill and practice come into play.

Many times you can only see part of the squirrel. The squirrel may just have its head sticking around the back side of the tree trunk or the squirrel might have half of its body covered by leaves.

Now is when you need to decide whether or not to take the shot. If you have a shot at the squirrel, regardless of how small of a portion of the squirrel it might be, you need to decide if this is going to be your best opportunity to shoot this squirrel.

Shot Placement

Now that a squirrel is in shooting range let's discuss where you should attempt to place your shot. If possible, the best place to hit the squirrel is in the head, which will provide a very quick and lethal kill.

Reasons for shooting in the head:

- Most humane shot for a kill
- Preserves the most meat

Squirrels are very small animals so it is important to be conscious of your shot placement in order to preserve most of the meat. It can be tempting to shoot the squirrel in the body because that is a much larger target to hit. However, if you want a chance at getting much meat off the squirrel you should try for a head shot.

Improving Shot Accuracy

One of the best ways to drastically improve your shooting accuracy is to have a stable surface to rest against when you shoot. This helps to keep you from swaying back and forth which will create inaccurate shots. It is surprising how difficult it is to stand still and aim effectively without bracing yourself.

How to take better shots:

- Lean against the side of a tree
- Kneel down and rest your elbow on your knee
- Take a deep breath just before you shoot

All three of the above methods are excellent ways that I have used to take better shots at squirrels. My preference is leaning against the side of a tree as I shoot. If you are hunting in the woods you should not have much difficulty finding a nearby tree to lean against as you shoot.

Kneeling is a good option if there is not another tree nearby that is convenient to lean against. However, in most situations there will be plenty of trees around to use as your stabilizer.

Finally, to stabilize your shot you want to take a deep breath just before you shoot. Breathing causes the gun to move up and down. As you get into shooting position and are just about ready to take your shot, take a deep breath. Then aim and slowly let your breath out. You should find that this technique greatly improves the accuracy of your shots.

Learn From Missed Shots

Any squirrel hunter, whether they are experienced or not, has missed shots at squirrels. It is important not to get down on yourself when you miss. Squirrels are very fast and often are in trees with thick leaves and branches.

Use missed shots as an opportunity to learn from your mistakes. Try to evaluate what you did well and what you could have done differently. Did you use something to brace yourself for an accurate shot? Did you allow the squirrel to get into a clear opening if possible? Did you shoot too soon? These are all questions to ask yourself in order to improve your shooting success.

Over time, your hit rates will improve, but keep in mind that it is tough to have 100% accuracy and that is completely okay and normal.

Keep reading to learn how to retrieve the squirrel you just shot...

Step 19: Retrieving Your Squirrel

You Hit the Squirrel, Now What?

After you shoot a squirrel you will want to retrieve your game. Use these tips to have success retrieving your squirrel.

Tips after shooting:

- Note where the squirrel lands
- Walk slowly to the squirrel
- Check to ensure the squirrel is dead before you grab it

Note Where the Squirrel Lands

If you shoot a squirrel that is in a tree it will often fall from the spot where it was and drop to the ground. The good news is that finding squirrels that you have shot is usually not very difficult. But to ensure you can locate it, pay attention to where it lands.

Look for any landmarks that are near where it fell. For example, pick out another small tree or bush in the area that you can use as a landmark to walk to. Depending on the area you are hunting, the leaves and undergrowth can cover up the squirrel and make it difficult to find unless you have a way remember the exact spot where it landed.

Walk Slowly to the Squirrel

While you walk to the spot where the squirrel is lying, it is important to proceed slowly. Sometimes you may have just wounded the squirrel so you want to keep an eye on the ground to look for any movement. On the off chance the squirrel is still alive and moving across the ground, it may be necessary to shoot it again.

The other reason you want to walk slowly to the squirrel is to look for any other squirrels in the immediate area. It is not uncommon for more than one squirrel to be in the same tree so even though you shot one squirrel there may still be others left behind that you could also shoot.

Check to Ensure the Squirrel is Dead Before You Grab It

Before you pick up the squirrel it is very important to ensure that the squirrel is dead. If you pick up a squirrel that is still alive the chances are you will get bitten. In most cases, particularly if you shoot the squirrel in the head, it will die immediately. However, do not take any chances and do a quick test just to be sure.

An easy way to do this is by grabbing a stick that is on the ground and poking the squirrel to see if it moves. If it shows any movement at all you need to quickly finish off the squirrel.

To do this, step on the squirrel's body with your boots to pin the squirrel down and then take out your hunting knife and cut the throat and neck area of the squirrel. This is never a fun task, but it is important to treat the squirrel humanely and alleviate any suffering as soon as possible.

Keep reading to learn how to clean the squirrel you just shot...

Step 20: Squirrel Cleaning

Success! You Retrieved Your Squirrel. Now What?

Once you bagged your squirrel it is time to clean it. It is important to prepare your squirrel to take home soon after shooting it, especially if it is a hot day outside. This is because the internal organs of the squirrel can actually cause the meat to spoil quickly. So try to clean it out as soon as possible.

Note: This will get messy. Some people purchase disposable plastic gloves to try to stay as clean as possible.

Steps to Clean Your Squirrel:

Here I will walk you through how to clean your squirrel. You might also want to view this video I found that will help you visualize this process at https://youtube/BZB7iE2b21M.

STEP 1: Cut through the squirrel's tail and fur but be sure not to cut the tail off. Do this by using your knife to cut from just behind the tail with a cutting motion that is towards it back. You do not want to cut from the top of the tail back. Ensure that you cut all of the way through the tail bone but again not all of the way through the hide on the other side.

STEP 2: Use your thumb and knife to open up this area around the tail a little further. Do this by pulling back on the tail slightly and cutting a little more of the skin and fur towards each side of the squirrel's body. Do this until you have about a 3-4 inch section opened up.

STEP 3: Now step on the tail and with your hands, grab the hind legs and pull up. All of the fur will stay on the ground by your foot and the skinned squirrel will be exposed. Keep pulling until the fur is all of the way down to the elbow joints of the squirrel.

STEP 4: While continuing to step on the tail, grab the remaining fur on the back quarter of the squirrel and pull it back until it is folded back over the joint in the hind legs.

STEP 5: Grab the hind leg area and hold the squirrel tightly extended with your foot still on the tail and cut the front legs by their joints. This will leave about half of the squirrel's legs on the body and it will also separate the hide completely from the legs.

Comment [JM]: Confusing – I would think you'd want to say something like "Lay the squirrel on its back and make a cut just in front of where the tail connects to the body going across the width of the body."

STEP 6: While continuing to hold the back legs and step on the tail, cut the squirrel's head off at the base of the neck. When you do this it will cut off the head and the entire hide section that you had been stepping on with your foot.

STEP 7: Now take your knife and cut off the hind legs around the joints. This will release the last quarter of the fur and will leave you a completely skinned squirrel.

STEP 8: Now it is time to cut the rib cage/sternum of the squirrel. While holding the squirrel with one hand with its belly facing up, cut through the middle of the ribs/sternum by working from the bottom of the rib cage up to the neck area.

STEP 9: Now rotate the squirrel in your hand 180 degrees so the hind legs are now facing away from you and split the squirrel open. Do this by starting your knife in the cut that you used to open up the ribs/sternum and work it back all of the way to its hind legs. Be sure that you are just cutting the skin open while ensuring not to go too deep into the cavity of the squirrel where you might puncture internal organs. Once it is cut all of the way, pull the thighs apart until you hear the pelvic bone crack open.

STEP 10: Now reach into the neck section and grab the air pipe of the squirrel and pull out all of the insides of the squirrel, working them back to the tail section of the squirrel. Ensure the intestines and all organs are removed.

STEP 11: You can now rinse off the squirrel and prepare it for how you like to eat it.

Now let's discuss how to cook your squirrel...

Step 21: Time to Enjoy Your Squirrel!

Preparing a Simple Yet Delicious Squirrel Dish

A great thing about the sport of squirrel hunting is that it not only provides joy and excitement while you are out hunting, but it also provides an incredible meal when you are done with your hunting trip.

I find it very satisfying to share the game I shoot with friends and family. The flavor of squirrel is unique and it is a great conversation piece as you sit around the dinner table.

The good news is that you can cook the squirrel you shot in a very simple way that turns out incredibly good. Preparation time for the meal is just a few minutes and the ingredients are minimal and common around the house.

How to Fry Squirrels

What you need:

- 1 Fresh shot squirrel, cut into 5 pieces

- Flour

- Seasoned salt

- Canola oil

- Frying pan with high edges

- Large Tupperware-style storage container

- Kitchen tongs

- Paper towels

STEP 1: Add 1 cup of flour and 4 tablespoons of seasoned salt to the inside of your Tupperware-style storage container.

STEP 2: Close the lid and shake up the flour and salt until the two ingredients are mixed together well.

STEP 3: Open up the storage container and place the squirrel pieces inside. Close the lid and shake the container for about 10-15 seconds until the pieces are covered on all sides with the flour and salt mixture.

STEP 4: Place your frying pan on the stove and pour about 1 inch of oil into the bottom of the pan. Turn the heat to medium-high and allow it to preheat for approximately 5 minutes.

STEP 5: Use kitchen tongs to take the squirrel pieces and gently place them in the hot oil. As you place the meat in the oil, let the bottom of each piece touch the pan first and then gently place the rest of the meat down in a direction away from you. By placing the meat down away from you it will help keep the hot oil from splashing back onto you.

STEP 6: Let the meat cook for 2-3 minutes on the first side and then flip the meat over using your kitchen tongs. You will know when the meat is ready when the first side is golden brown.

STEP 7: After both sides of the squirrel have been cooked to a golden brown color place the squirrel pieces on a plate that is covered with about 2-3 paper towels. Having the paper towels on the plate will help soak up the excess oil.

STEP 8: Sprinkle a little of the seasoned salt on both sides of the meat to your personal taste.

STEP 9: Allow the squirrel to cool for about 5 minutes and then enjoy the meal that you shot.

Final Words

Congratulations! You have taken your first step in becoming a successful squirrel hunter.

Make Sure to Enjoy Yourself

Regardless of the success you have, make sure you enjoy the time you spend outdoors.

Practice Makes Perfect

Getting started with anything can be challenging at first. Think back to when you first started tying your shoes. At first it was difficult, but after time it became second nature. This can be the same with squirrel hunting. The more you do it, the better you will get.

Make Progress Every Day

Using the steps learned in this book will help improve your squirrel hunting skills. I encourage you to make some type of progress each day of the season. Keep reading books, following hunting blogs, and watching YouTube videos. Six months from now you will be surprised how far you have made it by spending time learning more about squirrel hunting each day.

Made in the USA
Columbia, SC
29 December 2020